SPEED READING MADE EASY
Read Faster, Remember More
Improve Your Comprehension

Kathleen L. Hawkins
The Speed Reading Expert

ISBN-13: 978-0-9745452-4-0
ISBN-10: 0-9745452-4-4

1. Speed reading 2. How to speed read 3. How to read faster
4. Improve your reading speed and comprehension
5. Remember what you read 6. Kathleen L. Hawkins, speed-reading expert I. Title

Windsor Westcott
❖ **Publishing** ❖
(817) 768-8332

Rave Reviews from Graduates of Speed Reading Made Easy

(the course on which this book is based)

EXAR

Makes Analog and Mixed-signal ICs for Video, Imaging, and Communications Markets

We found a speed-reading course that works! – Director of Human Resources

The best in-house class I've ever taken. I'd absolutely recommend it. It covered a good deal of content in digestible chunks that I was able to understand. I more than doubled my reading rate.

I now read three times faster! This is a quick way to learn to be more productive. Outstanding. Useful ideas I can use every time I read.

EMC^2

Leading Content Management Provider for e-Business

Please find the course evaluations attached. These are very high marks. Thanks for a great class. – Training Coordinator

Kathleen is obviously VERY experienced in this area. She was well prepared and well organized and did an excellent job presenting the material in an easy-to-follow format. Speed reading is a valuable tool that will help me every day. I doubled my speed in 15 minutes!

A great course! All the participants doubled their speed and some increased three and four times.

GENENTECH

Founder of the biotechnology industry

Exceptionally helpful! I applied my new knowledge immediately. Very encouraging. Thanks for the self-confidence booster.

I learned exciting ways to think about reading that I can integrate easily into my business and personal life.

Anyone in school or business needs this course. Kathleen changed my traditional way of reading to a more comprehensive approach. I tripled my speed.

VISTAGE

An International CEO Membership Organization

Excellent! I improved 3 times and can't wait to finish the book. This'll help me get through my reading with enthusiasm and ease.

I highly recommend this course to anyone with a significant amount of reading.

The very easy techniques tripled my reading speed in a couple of hours. Reading has gone from being drudgery to being fun. I love it! Thanks again.

UNIVERSITY OF MICHIGAN

Stephen M. Ross School of Business
(BBAs, MBAs, and Executive MBAs)

I went from 330 to 1150 words per minute; pretty good! I wish I could get the same return on my stocks.

Fantastic! From 430 words per minute to more than 1,000 w.p.m. with very high retention. A great new approach to reading, surprisingly good, effective, and simple.

I wish that I'd had this information earlier in my academic career. I'd have cut my studying by 75% and had more time for other activities from day one. This class should be part of every MBA curriculum considering all the time pressure we're under.

An excellent workshop with immediate, practical benefits. I'm not a native speaker, but I improved my reading skills. I'll also use these techniques in my native language.

Kathleen's ideas brought about an instant change in my reading and comprehension. I was surprised by what I was able to remember as my words per minute tripled and my comprehension improved.

I've continued to work on the speed-reading techniques over the last month and can't believe how fast I'm processing information and content!

Also by Kathleen L. Hawkins

Books

The Insiders
We Know what You're Thinking
And the Truth will be Told

Spirit Incorporated
How to Follow Your Spiritual Path From 9 to 5
Whatever Your Job, Faith, or Challenge

Time Management Made Easy

Test Your Entrepreneurial I.Q.

Audio-learning Program

How to Organize Yourself to Win

Additional Resources

Free tips
SpeedReadingExpert.com/speed-reading-tips

Speed-reading software
WinningSpirit.com/speed-reading-software

Contents

Welcome to Speed Reading Made Easy

There's more reading to do today than ever before in history.

- If you were to read one book a week every week of your life, you would *not* have read 1/10 of 1% of the books in the New York Public library
- A weekday edition of the New York Times has more information in it than the average person in 17th Century England was likely to encounter in a lifetime
- You'd have to read day and night for more than 17 years to read everything that's published in one year alone—and that's *before* reading on the Internet, which basically goes on forever

If you have a heavy workload and lots of reading this book will be well worth your time. You'll learn techniques and strategies that you can use right away to be a faster, better reader online and offline in print media: newspapers, magazines, and books. In fact, one of the techniques has been proven to increase people's reading rates 50% or more as soon as they start to use it; many people actually double or triple their reading speed with this one technique alone. And you'll learn a lot of other techniques, as well.

Results

You'll learn how to increase your reading rates dramatically in all kinds of material while maintaining the same level of comprehension or increasing it—and remember more of what you read—by using the tips and strategies in this book.

The real deal

I'm Kathleen Hawkins, a speed-reading expert with a master's degree in reading education who has taught speed reading for years—in person—to more than 60,000 people with all kinds of reading from high-tech material to academic studies.

My students have been computer programmers, data management experts, executives, managers, attorneys, software designers, and aerospace engineers (yes, rocket scientists). And I taught speed reading to all the business students, MBA students, and Executive MBA students at the University of Michigan for 11 years. People from all levels of business, science, industry, and education are using what they learned in my course on which this book is based.

I'm also a writer who knows reading from the inside out—what makes material easy to read or more challenging—and I'll give you the strategies to deal with all of it.

It takes me a long time to write a book and, yet, I teach people how to read one in a few hours. Does it bother me to have people speed read the books I write? No, not at all. I write to share my ideas and expertise with others; the faster that people can read and understand what I write and apply it in their lives, the better. So please read this book quickly for good comprehension and enjoy.

Kathleen L. Hawkins
"The Speed Reading Expert"

Let's Begin

It's my goal to have you reading faster by page 14. Here's how we'll accomplish this.

Skimming and pacing hand motions
You'll learn to get a big picture—a preview—of what's going to be in any material that you're *about to read* by using sweeping hand motions on the pages. And then you'll learn tighter hand motions to pace yourself *as you read* for good comprehension. I'll give you two skimming techniques and two pacing techniques.

Comprehension
You'll have two kinds of comprehension tests: one I'll give you and the other will be a *self*-comprehension test. It's more useful ultimately to know how to test your own comprehension in any kind of material than it is to depend on others to tell you how well you're doing. I'll give you a great way to do this and reassure yourself that you got what you needed from the material.

Remember what you read—forever if you want
You'll experience an innovative way to take notes that you can use to replace your old way of taking notes or supplement the system you already use.

Use the techniques on fiction and nonfiction
You'll learn the techniques on fiction first and then apply them to nonfiction. So please find a practice novel with easy-to-read print, about 250-320 words on a page, such as a western, gothic, young-adult novel, or a romance. Why easy novels? Because when you learned to read you learned on easier books with large print. You had to learn to "walk" before you learned to "run"; same thing with speed reading.

You'll also need some nonfiction so please have some study, work-related, or business reading handy to practice your new skills. I'll give you additional tips and strategies to use with detailed material.

Please jot down the following on a separate piece of paper.

Record Sheet

First Read/Fiction (words per page: ___)
Novel: TITLE wpm ___ comprehension ___%

Final Read/Fiction (words per page: ___)
Novel: TITLE wpm ___ comp. ___%

Practice Reads ______________________

First Read/Nonfiction (327 words)
"Make a Habit of Getting Things Done" wpm ___ comp. ___%

Final Read/Nonfiction (405 words)
"The Flaws of Perfectionism" wpm ___ comp. ___%

~~~

Now please compute the words per page in your novel:

Compute the Words per Page (wpp) in Fiction

Open your novel to a *full* page of print—somewhere in the middle—and count the number of words in 3 *full lines* of print and divide by 3 to get the average words per line.

Then count the number of lines on a *full page* of print (a line with one word counts as a line, which keeps the math simpler) and multiply that by the average words per line.

Please write that number on your Record Sheet where it says "words per page" after "First Read/Fiction" and "Final Read/Fiction."
~~~

Test Your Beginning Speed and Comprehension in Fiction

You'll need two paperclips: one to mark off where you begin to read during a test, practice section, or a drill and one to mark where you stop reading (you need to know how much material you covered so you can compute your words per minute). You'll also need a stopwatch or a timer and a calculator. Once you have these items, please take a moment to see what your novel is about: read the front and back covers and any blurbs in the front material on the inside.

Next, turn to the beginning of the novel; it'll probably be part of a page, rather than a full page, and that's okay. Put a paperclip there and then read comfortably for 3 minutes as far as you can into the book for good comprehension.

Put the second paperclip next to the last sentence you read and then estimate your comprehension using the following guidelines. Choose a percentage and write that on your Record Sheet under First Read/ Fiction next to the title of your novel.

Comprehension Guidelines

- **High, 90-100%**: I'm satisfied with my understanding; I remember the plot or main idea and most or all of the details.
- **Medium, 66-89%**: I remember the plot or main idea and some of the details.
- **Low, 50-65%**: I remember the plot or main idea, but few details.
- **0-49%**: I saw and understood isolated words.

Then compute your reading rate: words per page times the pages you read = the total words you read. Divide that total by three (it was a 3-minute read) to get the total words per minute (wpm).

Portion of a page covered with print: ¼ a page = .25; ½ a page = .5; ¾ a page = .75

Examples: Two ½ pages = 1 page; two and ¾ a page = 2.75

Test Your Beginning Speed and Comprehension in Nonfiction

Give yourself as much time as you need to read the following article, "How to Make a Habit of Getting Things Done." Jot down the time you start to read and the time you finish. Then take the comprehension test that follows the article.

Time started: _______

How to Make a Habit of Getting Things Done
(324 words)

Some habits, such as waking up at a certain time in the morning and going to classes, are useful. Other habits, like being disorganized aren't productive and can be hard to change.

One obstacle to changing a habit is a desire to stay within a comfort zone. This might be why we procrastinate, let our workspaces get messy, or stick with other habits that are as familiar as old shoes. We hate to throw them away even though they're worn out. But those shoes were once new and uncomfortable until we got used to them. Likewise we must be willing to experience some discomfort at first while we grow into new and better ways of doing things.

On average it takes three weeks to break a habit. Allow yourself at least that long to replace your old behavior with more effective patterns. Choose one habit at a time to change, such as letting your work area get messy and change it now. Here's a plan:

1. Understand your habit. • List the ways you continue your habit • List the problems it causes • List the benefits of changing it.
2. Focus on the results you want. Instead of saying "I'm going to clean my workspace" say "I have a clean workspace."

3. Beware of slipping. The second you stray from your goal stop what you're doing and begin your new pattern. If you see clutter starting to accumulate, pick it up right away.
4. Exaggerate the results for three weeks. If you're messy, be extremely neat for the next three weeks to establish a new pattern.
5. Reward yourself as you go. If you want a clean work area, clean your desk first, then the bookcase, then streamline your files. Reward yourself after each completion.
6. Avoid using absolutes. Promising you'll *always* keep your work area neat doesn't allow for the unexpected. Be firm with yourself when you're changing a habit, but be reasonable as well.

Time finished: _______

Now take the comprehension test.
How to Make a Habit of Getting Things Done

1. Habits are easy to change. True False
2. Some habits are useful. T F
3. A block to breaking a habit is a desire to stay within a comfort zone. T F
4. Usually it takes a week to change a habit. T F
5. It's wise to break several habits at a time. T F
6. To help break a habit, write your goal in finished form. T F
7. When you catch yourself slipping back into old patterns stop what you're doing and practice your new behavior. T F
8. Exaggerate new behavior for three weeks to establish a new pattern. T F
9. Reward yourself only when you've completely broken the old habit. T F
10. When breaking a habit, promise to never slip back into old patterns. T F

Answers

1) F 2) T 3) T 4) F 5) F 6) T 7) T 8) T 9) F 10) F

Give yourself 10 points for each correct answer you checked and record your comprehension score on your Record Sheet, First Read/ Nonfiction.

Then compute your words per minute: 324 words divided by your time in seconds multiplied by 60 = words per minute (write your score on your Record Sheet, First Read/Nonfiction).

How fast do people read on average?
Most people read about 250 to 300 words a minute before they learn to speed read—and they *speak* about 250 to 300 wpm. If you read as fast as you talk, that means you're saying the words to yourself ("subvocalizing") as you read, which is probably the worst habit that slows you down. I'll give you several techniques to reduce subvocalizing, but first, let's look at how to increase your reading rate instantly when you use the following five strategies.

How to Increase Your Reading Rate—Instantly

There are five ways, when used in combination, that allow you to increase your reading rates instantly: skim before you read to get a preview, pace yourself as you read for good comprehension, reduce subvocalization, have good posture, and set time limits. Let's look at each of these.

1. Skim Before You Read to Get a Preview

Speed readers skim before they read because it's natural to get a big picture first and then to relate the details to the big picture. To demonstrate this for yourself, roll up a sheet of paper, close one eye and look at the room through the tube with the other eye. When you go into a room, is this the way you see it, one thing at a time? No. You see the whole room at a glance and *then* you notice the details (well, maybe some mornings when you go into the kitchen all you see is the coffee pot, but most of the time you see the whole room first, and then the details).

Too narrow a focus can give you incorrect information (like in life). To demonstrate this point to the students in my classes, I look through the tube at a few empty chairs—which I set aside before they came in—and I make incorrect assumptions: "There's no one here, they said the class would be full. People are probably caught in traffic." But in fact, the room is full of people.

Likewise, you grasp what you're reading more quickly when you relate the details to the big picture rather than start out cold and plod along word-by-word wondering where it's all headed.

Skimming before you read also gives you an idea if the material is going to be easy to read (because you're familiar with the subject and it's well written), more challenging and slow going (because the subject is new to you), or a combination (it's a familiar subject with some new concepts). Skimming helps you prepare to vary your speed throughout the material: slower on unfamiliar material, faster on easy material, and more leisurely to savor a particular section.

Road maps

Skimming before you read is a little like looking at a road map or Google Earth before you take a trip. If you know the lay of the land you can get a sense of where you can travel at top speed because the roads are straight and where you might need to slow down because of hills, turns, or big cities. You might also notice places where you'll want to allow more time to pull over and simply enjoy the scenery.

You'll also have an idea of where the material is going to end up and what the author covers, which helps you to read faster. It's similar to when you leave home for the day, if you don't know where you're going, how long will it take to get there? Quite a while, but if you know that you're going to work or the store or a friend's house, you go straight there.

How much should you skim?

Skim by chapter, article, or news story. Is there anything you wouldn't skim? I personally don't skim poetry because it's meant to be read out loud, and I wouldn't skim a "who-dun-it" novel, either, because then I'd find out who did, and then why read it? Skim novels for *practice*, though, but not if you're just reading for fun. Be sure to skim all work-related reading or study material before you read it. It'll save you time overall.

The trickiest words: negative words

Skim certain material *twice*, such as contracts, legal documents, and medical information. The first time you skim, look for negative words, like "no, can't, shouldn't, wouldn't," and "not." If you're reading offline, put a soft-lead pencil check in the margin next to them. This is to make you aware of the negatives because the human brain has trouble visualizing negatives and sometimes reads them as positives.

I saw a breakfast drink in a store, for example, and on the front of the carton in big letters were the words "Sugar Added." Were they bragging, especially these days when people are so health conscious? And then I saw the word "No" in front of "Sugar Added." I didn't notice it at first because my conscious brain didn't process the negative and, yet, I sensed that something didn't make sense and I reread it.

If negative words are hard to see, how can you be sure you'll see them when you skim ahead to look for them?

You'll see them because they'll be the *only* words for which you look on the first skim. For example, suppose you want to look up the last name "Harris" in a directory. You go to the "H" section and skim through all the names that begin with "H." Because you know what you're looking for, that'll be the name that jumps out at you. All the others are just "background."

So when you skim before you read, especially legal, medical, or complicated material, notice where the writer uses negatives. This increases your chances of reading it correctly. Then go back and skim a second time to get an idea of what's in the material, and then read it for good comprehension.

I'll give you the two skimming techniques later, but for now I'm just giving you a big picture of the five strategies.

2. Pace Yourself as You Read for Good Comprehension

Speed readers pace themselves on the page when they read, brushing along quickly and smoothly under each line with their hand—about 2 or 3 seconds a line—moving comfortably down the pages looking for ideas.

In my speed-reading classes we choose partners for a demonstration; one is "A" and the other "B." The "A"s imagine a large circle around their partners and follow the circle around with their eyes while the "B"s notice how jerky the "A"s eye motions look. Then the "B"s do the same thing, imagine a circle around their partners and follow it with their eyes.

People report that their partner's eye motions have a lot of angles. Some eye motions look like "w"s, other eye motions are more horizontal with points on the ends, and some look like scribbles—we joke that those people probably drank too much coffee that morning and are "wired" or ate too many sugar donuts before class and are experiencing a sugar "rush."

Then we repeat the demonstration, but this time each person follows the circle around with his or her own hand; people report that the second time their partner's eye motions are much smoother. The same is true when you use your hand as a guide on the page; your eye motions are smoother.

Searching and following

Our eyes have two kinds of motions: searching and following. When you *used* to read word-by-word, you plodded along on the page with jerky eye movements, but when you speed read, your hand guides your eyes smoothly and comfortably down the pages, which is easier on your eyes, and you also have the *feel* of the page. This helps you to concentrate, and when you concentrate, your comprehension improves.

Let's go to the car races

Before a race the cars follow a pace car around the track to line up in their starting positions and begin the race from a "rolling start" instead of a standing start. The drivers don't stare directly at the pace car or they'd run into each other. Instead, they keep moving their eyes, which expands their field of vision.

Same thing when you pace yourself on a page. Don't stare directly at each word or at your fingers; look at the lines a little *above* your moving fingertips on the page.

But maybe when you learned to read your teacher said, "Don't point at the words." That's excellent advice because if I said, "Look," and pointed with my finger, you'd look right where I was pointing. The same is true if you point at every word. Pointing causes you to focus on single words; that slows you down. When you speed read you relax your hand and move your fingers so quickly under the lines that you don't have time to focus on single words. Instead of using your finger as a pointer, you use several fingers as a guide.

Let's practice

Please turn to where you left off in your novel after the first 3-minute read where you put a paperclip. Leave that paperclip there; it now becomes the first paperclip marking the next section.

Then read for 3 minutes for good comprehension, as far as you can, into the new material. Brush your fingers along under each line as quickly as possible and still understand what you're reading.

At the end of 3 minutes, take the paperclip from the first page in the book and move it to where you just stopped reading so the two paperclips mark off the section you just read, compute your words per minute (wpm), and write that down on your Record Sheet where it says "Practice Reads."

~~~
~~~

Did you read faster the second time than when you took the first 3-minute timed read? I bet you did. Did you double or triple your reading rate?

Increase your reading rate 50% or more

Earlier I said you'd learn a technique that would increase your reading rate 50% or more as soon as you use it. That was it. When you brush along under the lines, your rate goes up. If you didn't read faster during that last practice it might be because you've never read this way before and maybe your hand distracted you, "*Hmmm*, I have a hangnail," or, "My skin is dry. I could use some hand lotion." But the more you practice, the more comfortable you get with the technique and pacing becomes second nature.

If your eyes move faster than your fingers, move your fingers faster. If your fingers speed ahead too fast, move them a little slower.

Let's experiment

Read for a few minutes—from where you left off after the practice read you just did (where you put the paperclip) and continue to use the brushing hand motion. Move the second paperclip to where you stopped reading so the paperclips mark off the section you just read. Then take your hand off the page, keep reading, and try to keep up the same pace.

~~~

What happened? You probably slowed way down when you stopped pacing. You'll speed up again when you start to pace again.

Reduce rereading

Pacing also reduces "regressions," rereading. When you *used* to read word-by-word you'd be plodding along and this very creative, active brain of yours didn't feel challenged and started to think about the weekend. And before you knew it, you'd be half way down page and so far off track you'd have to go back to the beginning and read it over again. It's estimated that people who read about 250 words a
~~~

minute regress as many as 20 times *a page*. In a 300-page book, that's about 6,000 times!

Speed readers reread, too, but a lot less. We move down the pages so quickly that our minds have less time to wander. We might think, "Wait, what was that guy's name again?" and pop back up to get the name, or some other information, and then move on quickly. Good concentration is a by-product of speed reading. And, when you concentrate, your comprehension goes up, so pace yourself when you read. If you understand everything you're reading, pace yourself faster and challenge yourself to understand at faster speeds.

Pacing also helps you have fewer "fixations"
Fixations are stops that last hundredths of a second along the line; they happen so fast that you're not even aware of it. While your brain understands the last bit of information, your eyes are usually a phrase or two ahead of what you're conscious of reading and already beginning to process the new information.

Prior to pacing yourself, you made about three to six fixations on a line, but when you pace, you take in larger visual "chunks" of information. With pacing you might only need a couple fixations per line, or if you're reading narrow columns, you might find that you can pace vertically down the columns.

Could you pace with a ruler or an index card?
It's probably better to use your hand as a guide. A ruler or index card covers the upcoming print. We're incredibly receptive as human beings and can read peripherally (to the sides and above and below our central point of vision) if all the words are visible. Our peripheral vision helps us anticipate what's coming, which in turn can help us to read faster.

But doesn't your hand on the page cover some of the words, too?
Yes, but it moves quickly in a different pattern and there are spaces between your fingers so fewer words are covered for less time than they would be with a ruler or an index card.

Could you put the card above the lines and move it downward?
Some people do that and like it. Experiment with your options and use the techniques that work the best for you.

Will you always pace yourself when you read?
Probably, although you might be able to read narrow columns faster than you can move your hand. In that case, just glance down the columns without using your hand or pace in a straight line down the columns instead of across them. Again, do what works best for you.

Do these techniques work on computer reading, too?
Yes. Once you can read print faster, you'll read faster on a computer, too, although you probably won't pace yourself on a full-size monitor. The smaller screens on tablets, laptops, and smartphones, however, make previewing and pacing easy. And eReaders have functions that advance the pages quickly for skimming and also let you choose the font size and how text is displayed on the screen. I like to format what I read into larger fonts and columns and then I can really zoom through it.

If you want some automated practice training your rapid perception and testing your comprehension at faster rates, you could use the software described at WinningSpirit.com/speed-reading-software.

If you purchase software from WinningSpirit.com, I get a referral commission, but it doesn't cost any more if you buy it there and I only recommend products I use myself so you'll be in good hands.

3. Reduce Subvocalization

"Subvocalizing" means saying the words to yourself as you read. If you subvocalize, you can only read as fast as you can talk, about 250 to 300 words a minute; your mouth puts the brakes on your brain. If you say the words to yourself, you've already seen and understood them, so in a sense you're reading them twice. When you speed read, the words bypass your mouth and go directly from your eyes to your brain.

It is possible to eliminate subvocalizing, but probably more realistic to reduce it significantly. You'll learn several techniques in this chapter to help you do that.

Why do people subvocalize?

Most of us, as children, were taught to read phonetically by learning how to sound out words, such as when a word contains a double vowel (ai, ea, oa) just pronounce the first vowel in the pair, and know that a "silent e" is just as it says, silent, but the vowel before the silent "e" should be pronounced, and so on. Phonics is a part-to-whole way of learning.

Many of us were also taught the "whole language" method of reading. We memorized whole words, analyzed them in context, and used them in stories.

The best approach to teaching reading is a combination of phonics *and* whole language.

Teachers also have children read out loud so the teachers can analyze where they need help figuring out the words. This method is fine—it worked for most of us when we were learning to read—but many adults still pronounce every word in their minds. They think that reading means to pronounce the words when it really means to get meaning from the text; and that can be done by sight.

Let's experiment

Continue to read from where you left off reading after the brushing exercise in your novel, but now fill your mind with another sound so you can't pronounce every word to yourself. Make a gentle humming sound (or if you meditate, you might want to say "Om" or "Aum" instead), and notice that you can see and understand some of the words without pronouncing them.

For 15 seconds, read, pace, and hum—and remember to breathe.

~~~

This might be a challenge at first because you're not used to reading, pacing, and making sounds all at the same time. But with practice, you'll begin to read by sight. **Note**: this is just a demonstration; *don't* hum every time you read. If you go back to the office and make noises while you read, people might think you're acting strange.

Now quickly reread the last page that you read in your novel, brushing as you go—no humming this time—and read it over and over until all you have to do is simply look at it and understand it. The more you read it, the more familiar it becomes, the less you say each word to yourself, and soon you're reading silently. This is how it *feels* to read silently and gives you an idea of the goal.

You condense information naturally

You're used to seeing and understanding without running a verbal commentary. When you look out the window, for example, you don't think in complete sentences and paragraphs with correct punctuation: "I see a blue sky with white, puffy clouds—they're probably cumulus clouds—people are walking by the window and cars are driving by on the road." If you think in words at all, you probably think abbreviated thoughts like "sky, puffy clouds, people walking, cars." Or you see the scene and simply understand it.

Likewise if you tell people about a movie you saw, do you start with "Once upon a time in a galaxy far, far away ..." or if you're telling them about a book you read, do you say, "It was a dark and stormy night ...." and then repeat the movie script or the text in the book
~~~

best
better
big
black
blue
both
brown
clean
cold
eight
every
five
four
full
funny
good
green
hot
kind
light
little
long
many
new
old
one
own
pretty
red
right
round
seven
six
small
some
ten
the
three
two
warm
white
yellow

Verbs
am
are
ask
ate
must
open
try
be
bring
call
pick
play
use
came
can
carry
come
please
pull
walk
could
cut
did
do
put
ran
want
does
done
don't
draw
read
ride
was
drink
eat
fall
find
run
said
wash
fly
found
gave
get
saw
say
went
give
go
goes
going
see
shall
were
got
grow
had
has
show
sing
will
have
help
hold
hurt
sit
sleep
wish
is

jump	let	made
keep	like	make
know	live	may
start	take	think
stop	tell	write
work	would	
laugh	look	

The 150 Most Frequently Used Words

As with the Basic Sight Vocabulary list, these are also words that you should be able to see and know without having to pronounce to yourself.

1. the
2. of
3. and
4. a
5. to
6. in
7. is
8. you
9. that
10. it
11. he
12. was
13. for
14. on
15. are
16. as
17. with
18. his
19. they
20. I
21. at
22. be
23. this
24. have
25. from
26. or
27. one
28. had
29. by
30. word
31. but
32. not
33. what
34. all
35. were
36. we
37. when
38. your
39. can
40. said
41. there
42. use
43. an
44. each
45. which
46. she
47. do
48. how
49. their
50. if
51. will
52. up
53. other
54. about
55. out
56. many
57. then
58. them
59. these
60. so
61. some
62. her
63. would
64. make
65. like
66. him
67. into
68. time
69. two
70. more
71. write
72. go
73. number
74. no
75. way

76. my
77. than
78. first
79. water
80. been
81. call
82. who
83. oil
84. has
85. look
86. could
87. people
88. now
89. find
90. long
91. down
92. day
93. did
94. get
95. come
96. made
97. many
98. part
99. over
100. new
101. sound
102. take
103. only
104. little
105. work
106. know
107. place
108. year
109. live
110. me
111. back
112. give
113. most
114. very
115. after
116. thing
117. our
118. just
119. name
120. good
121. sentence
122. man
123. think
124. say
125. great
126. where
127. help
128. through
129. much
130. before
131. line
132. right
133. too
134. mean
135. old
136. any
137. same
138. tell
139. boy
140. following
141. came
142. want
143. show
144. also
145. around
146. form
147. three
148. small
149. set
150. put

Most of what you read is made up of simple words

Thirty to sixty percent of what you read today is made up of words that come from the previous two lists of words. This is true of all the material I've studied so far, including detailed material. Here are some examples: The Wall Street Journal 41%; article on management and supervision 44%; finance text 41%; engineering text 38%; a book I wrote *Spirit Incorporated* 50%.

In fact, the first 25 words on the "150 Most Frequently Used Words" list make up one-third of the reading material in English.

1. the
2. of
3. and
4. a
5. to
6. in
7. is
8. you
9. that
10. it
11. he
12. was
13. for
14. on
15. are
16. as
17. with
18. his
19. they
20. I
21. at
22. be
23. this
24. have
25. from

Simple words don't necessarily mean the ideas are simple
Authors can write about complex ideas and issues using clear, simple vocabulary. Ernest Hemingway, known for his economy of language, won the Pulitzer Prize in 1953, for his classic story, *Old Man and the Sea*. A year later he received the Nobel Prize in Literature.

Read for Ideas

To reduce subvocalization, read for ideas; just subvocalize the key words: nouns (people, places, and things), and verbs (action words). What's the following sentence about? **The beautiful _____ _____ the _______.**

You can't tell because "The beautiful the" aren't key words. They don't carry the meaning of the sentence. Here's the complete sentence: **The beautiful rainbow spanned the mountains.** What are the key words? **rainbow spanned mountains**. It's twice as fast to say "rainbow spanned mountains" as it is to say "The beautiful rainbow spanned the mountains."

Don't you need to read *all* the words before you decide which ones are the key words?

You don't need to *say* every word to yourself. Reading means to get meaning from the text; you can do that by sight as you look for the key ideas. If you subvocalize just the key ideas, your mind should see and register the connecting words (the little words that make up one-third of the words in the English language).

Here's an excerpt (276 words) from my book *Spirit Incorporated.* Please skim the selection before you read it.

Language Shapes Our Experiences

The earliest lesson many of us learn when we first become interested in self-improvement is to express ourselves in positive terms. This is because the language we use, which reflects our beliefs, helps to shape our experiences. Being positive also serves us in the workplace where we want to encourage cooperation, make sales, serve customers well, produce quality products, and make a profit.

It's important to note, however, that some casual negative comments are just that, casual and innocent. "This cheesecake is to die for!" for example, uses the idiom, "to die for" to mean, "Incredibly delicious, the best I've ever eaten!" This is probably a fairly harmless statement although some health-food enthusiasts might think it's prophetic.

On the other hand, some negative comments that appear to be casual on the surface are actually fueled by negative emotions. These kinds of negatives, used on a regular basis, can produce unwanted results. The comment, "They're filthy rich," for example, could mean that the speaker is envious of someone else, or might be thinking, "At least *someone* can make that kind of money; it may not be *me*, but *someone* can!" This is a strong, pessimistic affirmation, which, if used over time, could interfere with the speaker's financial success.

So the challenge for you is to notice which of the negatives you use are casual and innocent, and which are produced by strong negative emotions, "negative" because they might sabotage your success. Also notice if these negatives are part of an ongoing pattern of negativity. If this is the case, you might want to put a more positive spin on your communication.

~~~

Here's the same section with the key words underlined:

Language Shapes Our Experiences

The earliest lesson many of us learn when we first become interested in self-improvement is to express ourselves in positive terms. This is because the language that we use, which reflects our beliefs, helps to shape our experiences. Being positive also serves us well in the workplace where we want to encourage cooperation, make sales, serve customers well, produce quality products, and make a profit.

It's important to note, however, that some casual negative comments are just that .... casual and innocent. "This cheesecake is to die for!" for example, uses the idiom, "to die for" to mean, "Incredibly delicious, the best I've ever eaten!" This is probably a fairly harmless statement although some health-food enthusiasts might think that it's prophetic.

On the other hand, some negative comments that appear to be casual on the surface are actually fueled by negative emotions. These kinds of negatives, used on a regular basis, can produce unwanted results. The comment, "They're filthy rich," for example, could mean that the speaker is envious of someone else, or might be thinking, "At least *someone* can make that kind of money; it may not be *me*, but *someone* can!" This is a strong, pessimistic affirmation, which, if used over time, could interfere with the speaker's financial success.

So the challenge for you is to notice which of the negatives you use are casual and innocent, and which are produced by strong negative emotions, "negative" because they might sabotage your success. Also notice if these negatives are part of an ongoing pattern of negativity. If this is the case, you might want to put a more positive spin on your communication.

~~~

And here's the same selection (103 words) with the key words only (it's twice as fast to read the following article—and still retain the meaning—as it was to read the first version of the article):

Language Shapes Experiences

Earliest lesson many learn when interested in self-improvement is to express ourselves in positive terms. Language reflects beliefs, helps shape experiences. Being positive serves well in workplace … encourage cooperation, make sales, serve customers well, produce quality products, make money.

Some casual negative comments are innocent. "Cheesecake to die for!" "Delicious!" fairly harmless statements.

Some negatives appear casual, but fueled by negative emotions, used on regular basis can produce unwanted results. "They're filthy rich," speaker is envious … pessimistic affirmations could interfere with financial success. Notice which negatives are innocent, which produced by negative emotions, might sabotage success. Put positive spin on communication.

###

But little words can be important; you don't want to miss anything

Yes, they can be important. That's the beauty of skimming *before* you read. You get an idea of what's in the material and then go back and read at whatever speed you need to read according to your purpose for reading. If the consequences are serious if you miss a word, then read word-by-word if you need to. I read my first book contract word-by-word, for example, and even hired a literary agent to understand it for me. I wasn't familiar with many of the terms. I read my second book contract faster and the third and fourth book contracts the fastest of all—I even negotiated them myself.

The most frequently used word in the English language
What's **the** most frequently used word in **the** English language? It's **the** word "**the**." That's one of those words you can see and know without having to pronounce. **Note**: just because you don't say **the** "**the**"s to yourself, and you don't say **the** other little words, doesn't mean you're not reading them. Reading is **the** act of getting meaning from **the** text, which you can do without saying every "**the**."

When you subvocalize just the key words, you're "idea reading," you read in "chunks," or visual "gulps." In the example, "The beautiful rainbow spanned the mountains," a "chunk" or a visual "gulp" would be: **rainbow spanned mountains**. "Rainbow" and "mountains" are nouns and "spanned" is a verb.

If we don't need all the words, why do writers write them?
Text is like a filmstrip composed of many frames—each frame is needed to tell the story—but you don't watch a movie frame by frame and see each one in isolation. The filmstrip runs rapidly through a projector and the story unfolds seamlessly in front of you. Likewise you run the words in a story quickly through your brain and watch the story unfold seamlessly before you.

The Summarizing Technique

Another technique to use to teach yourself to stop subvocalizing (saying every word to yourself) when you read is to use the Summarizing Technique. Talk out loud (or talk to yourself if there are other people around) about what you're reading *while* you're reading. *Don't* read word-by-word, just summarize. You enjoyed humming earlier (yeah, right) so I thought you might enjoy this variation.

As your speed increases, summarizing might slow you down because you'll be reading by sight instead of by sound, so welcome the shift. That's when you'll really soar through the pages.

The "Say-Another-Word" Technique

Another way to stop saying every word to yourself is to repeat a word while you read, such as "focus," "understand," or "concentrate."

A graduate of my speed-reading class said this: "I tried to apply the 'Say-Another-Word' technique and always found myself eventually saying the words on the page one by one in my mind. I got frustrated, stopped for a minute, and said: 'sound something as you read, Kathleen says this can work,' so I started to hum one of my favorite songs. It works! I started to see the words pass by and I didn't have to voice each one in my mind any more. I'll keep using this technique."

Your goal is to reduce subvocalization and depend on it less, *not* eliminate it entirely. Many highly skilled speed readers still subvocalize to various degrees. People also tell me that they subvocalize more in some kinds of material than in other kinds.

So, to reduce subvocalizing:

1. **Idea Read**. Just subvocalize the key words and ideas, which contain the message: nouns (people, places, and things) and verbs (action words).

2. **Summarize** to yourself while you read. As you read faster and faster, you'll probably summarize less and less.

3. **Say another word**. Silently repeat another word as you read, such as "focus," "concentrate," or "understand." **Note**: this can be challenging. Just do it for short periods of time while you're practicing—unless you get really good at it, enjoy it, and it works well for you.

4. **Train your rapid perception**. Flip through a magazine, close it, and remember the words and pictures you saw. Chances are you'll understand more than you thought, and the little voice in your mind will be quieter.

You're in the driver's seat

Your results with the speed-reading techniques will vary depending on how much you practice, what you already know about a subject, and your purpose for reading.

If you're highly accountable to know the material, skim it first and then go back and read at whatever speed you need to read in order to understand and assimilate it.

4. Have Good Posture

Do you read while you eat? Do you read in the bathtub—or in the *vicinity* of the bathtub? Do you read in bed at night until you fall asleep?

It's okay to read in all those places, I do sometimes, but when I do, my rates tend to drop. When you read and eat at the same time, your attention is divided between the book and your food and it's hard to pace yourself on the page with a fork in your hand. When you read in the tub, you might drop your book in the water. And, if you read in bed before you fall asleep, you're using reading as a tranquilizer (which is better than some things you could take). Just remember to remove the "fall asleep" suggestion the next day when you read for work or school. Instead, say, "I'm alert and focused and I get my reading done in record time with excellent comprehension."

To be a faster reader, don't get too comfortable. Sit in a straight-backed chair at a desk or table with the book at about a 45° angle. This makes the pages easy to see and it's a statement that you mean business; you're going to finish your reading in record time with great comprehension.

5. Set Time Limits on Your Reading

One way to read faster is to set time limits. The human mind is virtually limitless, so we need to set goals and deadlines to make progress. In my speed-reading classes I get the students to read faster because they know that I'm going to time them with a stopwatch. I say, "Get ready, begin!" and they burn through the pages, and then I say, "Stop."

They read faster because they have a beginning and an end, a tight deadline, which keeps them focused at the faster speeds. Without a time limit their reading rate would slow down.

Have you ever noticed how much longer things take when you have all the time in the world to do them and how much more you get done with a looming deadline?

To practice reading with time limits, you can use your own timer if you're reading offline or use the speed-reading software if you have it: WinningSpirit.com/speed-reading-software.

How to set time limits and deadlines on your reading

1. Give yourself a tight time limit on something you're about to read. If it's something you read on a regular basis, like a company report or a monthly magazine and it usually takes, say, about an hour to read, give yourself half that time.
2. Divide a big book into manageable sections and write a day or date for finishing each section on sticky tabs; place them accordingly throughout the book.
3. Be a SPIFy reader: read for **S**hort **P**eriods of **I**ntense **F**ocus, **y**es! Read flat out for 10 or 15 minutes, pacing as you read, and then stop and think about what you read; you'll read faster in that short time segment than if you just read until you wind down. Then continue to read for another 10 or 15 minutes and so on.

If you set a time limit, and it's your goal to finish an article or chapter within the time frame, but you still have a couple pages to go, read to the end, to a natural stopping place, for a sense of closure.

~~~

And there you have it, five strategies, when used in combination, that will increase your reading rates instantly: skim before you read, pace yourself as you read, reduce subvocalization, have good posture, and set time limits.
~~~

Comprehending Comprehension

In most cases, when reading speed increases, comprehension also increases. Reading two or three times faster helps you to focus your attention whereas your thoughts tend to wander at slower speeds, which makes rereading necessary.

We're a test-taking culture

We take about 3,625 tests, quizzes, midterms, and major exams during our academic years, which can cause us to look outside ourselves for validation. Knowing how to test our own comprehension helps us to pass the tests required to satisfy "scorekeepers," such as teachers, professors, or bosses and then to apply the information in other situations, as well, if we need to.

The best comprehension test

Tell someone about what you read. If you don't have anyone who wants to listen, make someone up—maybe an imaginary friend your parents tried to make you get rid of when you were a little kid—or tell an animal companion; dogs in particular love the attention.

You could also report to yourself. Turn to the table of contents in a book you've read and report from that or speak from the subtitles, the index, or the glossary. You'll know right away what you remember and what you need to read again. If you can talk about it, you know it. If you draw a blank, you know where you need to go back and study some more.

When I was studying for my master's degree, I had to take a two-hour final exam during which time three professors could ask me any questions they wanted about my three chosen authors. One of the professors had studied one of my authors for 15 years, so I felt a lot of pressure to know the material thoroughly. To prepare, I "rehearsed." I imagined sitting in the room talking to the professors. I turned to the table of contents in the books and spoke from those.

I'm happy to say I passed my exam and received my master's degree.

How to Improve Your Comprehension in Business and Study Material

It's more effective to read nonfiction several times quickly and layer your comprehension—understanding more on each consecutive read—than it is to read it through once, cold, from the beginning to the end. So skim first, ask yourself what you need from the material, and then go back and read it to answer your questions. And realize that these factors can affect your reading rate and comprehension: your entry level, purpose for reading, and interest in the material.

Your entry level

Your familiarity with the material can determine how fast you read. I have clients—geneticists, software designers, engineers, and attorneys—who will always read their respective material faster than I could because I'm not familiar with the concepts and terms. My entry level is low in that kind of material.

Your purpose for reading

Let your purpose for reading—to get an update, learn a skill, read for fun, or pass a course—determine your level of comprehension: remember in depth (about 90-100%), for fun (60-85%) or just be aware the material exists if you might need it again (20-30%).

Your interest in the material

Do you resist reading boring material? If that's the case, you might want to speed up and get through it quickly.

How to Improve Your Concentration and Focus

1. Skim before you read to get a preview of what's going to be in the material.

2. Be a SPIFy reader described on page 32. Divide your reading into sections with time limits for finishing each section.

3. Stay positive and upbeat: "I read quickly and comfortably … I focus well … my comprehension is great … I finish my reading in record time and remember what I read."

4. Jot a note to yourself if something pops into your mind and interrupts you while you're reading; then return quickly to your reading, confident that you'll remember what you need to remember later.

5. Keep your workspace clean and organized. Clutter can distract you.

6. Read with a purpose. Turn subtitles into questions. For example, turn the subtitle "The Best Way to …." into "What's the best way to …." and then read with the intention of answering the question.

7. Read to natural stopping places—to the ends of articles, stories, and chapters—rather than stopping midway.

The Skimming Hand Motions for Previewing The "Wave" and the "Slant"

As a speed reader you pace yourself on the page because you have an automatic response to motion and you get used to faster speeds.

An automatic response to motion is based on early survival instincts. Our forest-dwelling ancestors sat around crackling fires at twilight and something moved in the shadows—a wild animal, a lion, a tiger? If they didn't respond to the motion, they might have been killed.

You have the *same* response today (even though it's not likely that a tiger is going to jump out at you). If someone walked into the room, you'd glance up. As a speed reader you capitalize on this response by pacing yourself on the page. Your eyes are drawn to the motion, which helps you to increase your concentration and comprehension.

Another reason we pace ourselves is because we get used to faster speeds. Has this ever happened: you're heading out of town on a weekend, there's not much traffic, and your speedometer says 85 or maybe 90 miles an hour?

And then, on the horizon, you see a police car! What do you do? You slow down and now it probably feels like you're crawling along. This is because you got used to the faster speeds. When you speed read you get used to faster speeds, too, and after a while you'll be impatient with the slower speeds.

The "Wave"

You can practice this now on your novel. Start at the top of a page and move your hand back and forth down the page—a little like a waterfall flows downward—from top to bottom, taking about 5 or 6 seconds a page. Pick up any information you can. Look for key words, phrases, who, what, when, where, and why. Skim for one minute into your novel using the Wave technique.

~~~
~~~

Skimming might be a challenge at first because you're not used to moving so quickly on a page and might just see occasional words. But as you continue to practice, you pick up more and more information. Make a point to notice something in every paragraph. In nonfiction especially pay extra attention to the beginnings of paragraphs where you'll find the main idea about 68% of the time, and to the endings where you'll find it about 23% of the time.

The "Slant"

With your hand in a relaxed position make diagonals down the pages of your novel—left to right or right to left, whichever is most comfortable—about 5 or 6 diagonals a page—looking for any information you can pick up. You're *not* aiming for comprehension at this point. The more comfortable you get with this technique, and the more you practice, the more ideas you understand and the fewer slants you'll need to make on a page. You can practice this now in your novel: skim for 1 minute into the book using the Slant skimming technique.

~~~

If the columns are narrow you might be able to simply move your hand down the middle of the column and get a good idea of what's in the material.

Remember: skim first and then go back and read for comprehension. **Note**: there's a difference between speed reading and speed drills. Drills are designed to make you skim faster than you feel comfortable (they train you for speed before comprehension). If you understand the general idea during a drill, then go even faster to challenge yourself.

At first, notice whatever you can: a word or two here or there. You might understand more words and phrases on the tops of pages than the bottoms (or the other way around), or understand more on the right pages than on the left. Look for who, what, when, where, why, and how. Make it a goal to understand something in every paragraph.
~~~

Eventually, with practice, you could begin to understand whole sentences at a time. I personally find that sometimes I'm so relaxed while I'm skimming because I know that I'll be going back to read for comprehension that I get everything I need from the material just from skimming.

Let's do some drills

Set your timer for 1 or 2 minutes and skim as far as you can (starting from the last paperclip) into your practice novel using the "Wave" or the "Slant."

Return to where you began to skim (where the paperclip is) and read for 5 or 10 minutes into the book brushing along quickly and comfortably under the lines (it's okay to pass the point where you stopped skimming). Put the second paperclip next to the sentence where you stopped reading so the two paperclips mark off the section you just read.

Rest your eyes, think about what you read, and repeat from where you left off, skimming first for 1 or 2 minutes further into the book and then reading what you skimmed (again, it's okay to read past the point where you stopped skimming). Move forward like that through the book. When you finish one book, start another.

~~~

In addition to regular practice periods, you can train your rapid perception by making skimming a separate activity by itself. Skim an easy book or a magazine—maybe while you're waiting for a meeting to start or waiting in line—then close it and ask yourself what you remember.

Skim every day for 5 or 10 minutes, just to practice skimming and condition your mind to faster speeds.
~~~

The Role of Closure in Speed Reading

Closure is the tendency to complete a letter, figure, or a word, given minimal details. In the speed-reading classes we read the following out loud as a group:

> **You can under_tand what you're read_ng even when some of the let_ers or some of ___ w_rds are mis_ing.**

And everyone gets 100% comprehension even though part of the sentence is missing. You don't need every word to understand what's being said. Here's a longer section to see that this works with longer passages, too.

The Bushel Basket

> A man and a woman owned — country store where they sold grain in bulk. They had — bushel basket with a false bottom — it. When customers measured — grain, they unknowingly received less than — expected.
>
> One day the couple attended — inspiring lecture. The speaker spoke about ethics. After — lecture the speaker asked the couple if they liked — message. The man — woman exchanged glances. The woman finally said, "We don't remember exactly what — said, but when we go home, we're going to burn — bushel basket."

If you can fill in the blanks when some of the words are missing, you should be able to glance at the connecting words that are really there and understand them without saying them.

The Reading Hand Motions for Good Comprehension "Brushing" and "Tapping"

After you skim a section using the Wave or Slant motion, read it for good comprehension using either the Brushing or Tapping technique.

Brushing

You've already been using the Brushing technique as you brushed along under the lines on the pages of your practice material. Typically you brush along under each line, but then as you read faster and understand more, you might find that you can brush along under every two or three lines and read whole sentences at a glance.

Let's practice

Open your practice novel to where you stopped reading after the last practice exercise (where the paperclip is). Now read for 3 minutes into your novel using the Brushing reading technique.

Move the second paperclip to where you stopped reading, compute your words per minute (wpm) in the section you just read (between the paperclips), and record that on your Record Sheet on the line: "Practice Reads."

~~~

Tapping

With this technique as you move down the pages, you tap once, twice, or three times within each line. This encourages you to have fewer eye fixations per line. Instead of reading word by word, take in several "chunks" of words at a time. A "chunk" will have at least one noun and a verb in it.

xxxxxxx**X**xxxxxxx**X**xxxxxxx**X**xxxxxxx
xxxxxxx**X**xxxxxxx**X**xxxxxxx**X**xxxxxxx

xxxxxxxxxx**X**xxxxxxxxx**X**xxxxxxxxxx
xxxxxxxxxx**X**xxxxxxxxx**X**xxxxxxxxxx

xxxxxxxxxxxxxxx**X**xxxxxxxxxxxxxxx
xxxxxxxxxxxxxxx**X**xxxxxxxxxxxxxxx
~~~

Let's practice

Read for 3 minutes using the Tapping reading technique as far as you can into the book (starting from where you placed the paperclip after your last practice read).

At the end of 3 minutes move the second paperclip to where you stopped reading (so you've marked off the section you just read), compute your words per minute for that section, and record that on your Record Sheet on the line: "Practice Read."

~~~

Which reading technique did you like best? You might find that Brushing works well on longer lines and Tapping works well on shorter lines. Use whichever one works the best for you.

Start a Branch Recall Pattern to take notes

On a separate sheet of paper draw a diagonal line from the lower left of the page to the upper right, or the lower right to the upper left (depending on whether you're left-handed or right-handed). Or you could draw a circle or a "sun" with branches or "rays" coming off it. Then draw five branches slanting up or down off the main "branch." Label the branches Who, What, When, Where, Why/How. Then draw branches slanting off each of those branches.

On the "Who" branches jot down the characters' names, on the "what" branches key words that tell what the characters are doing, "Where" the story takes place (location), "When" (time of day, year, period in history, etc.), and "Why/How."

Fill in the details you remember, using key words and short phrases. Slant them off the main branches like branches on a tree (if you were reading nonfiction, put the chapter titles on the branches and subtitles slanting off those, then more details slanting off those).

There are examples of branch recall patterns on pages 49 and 51.
~~~

Test Your Final Speed and Comprehension in Fiction

Let's see how much you've improved your speed and comprehension. Please open your novel to where you put the paperclip after you practiced the Tapping reading hand motion.

Read for 3 minutes for good comprehension as far as you can into your novel using Brushing or Tapping. At the end of 3 minutes, put the second paperclip where you left off (so you mark off the section that you just read, from where you started to where you ended).

Please estimate your comprehension for that section, compute your words per minute for that section, and record those on your Record Sheet under Final Read/Fiction.

~~~

Remember that to compute your words per minute (wpm), multiply the words per page (wpp) times the pages you read to get the total words you read and then divide that total by the number of minutes you read, which in this case would be 3.

Comparing your first read on your Record Sheet with the final read you just did, did you increase your reading rate? I bet you did. Think about how great you'll be with practice.

You can use these techniques to read harder material, too
Continue to practice and your rates and comprehension should go up in all kinds of material. Realize, too, that you'll have a variety of reading rates depending on the kinds of material you're reading and your purpose for reading. Anything you read faster is going to give you more time to spend on harder material. Later I'll give you strategies that are specifically designed to use with very detailed, challenging material.
~~~

Test Your Final Reading Speed and Comprehension in Nonfiction

Now read the following article quickly for good comprehension. Jot down the time you start to read and the time you finish. Then take the comprehension test that follows the article.

Time started: ______

The Flaws of Perfectionism

Do you worry about what others think of you? Measure your self-worth in terms of your achievements? Do things over and over to get them just right? If you answered "yes" to any of these questions you might be a perfectionist.

It's good to be interested in quality, but be fair with yourself as well. Striving for unrealistic goals can impair your creativity, cause tension between you and others, and waste time. Here are some ways to break the patterns of perfectionism:

- Recognize the point of diminishing returns. When the return on your invested time begins to diminish, stop. When a report is written, for example, don't waste a day looking for a quote that might enhance it, but which isn't necessary.
- Realize that "below average" to a perfectionist is often perfectly acceptable to others.
- Let your purpose for doing a job determine how much time you spend on it. When you read for fun, don't aim for 100% comprehension.
- Work on trivia as little as possible. What's the least work you can do on something and still have it be acceptable?

- Delegate. If you believe for work to be done right you have to do it yourself, you might be denying others opportunities to grow. And you waste time trying to do everything yourself. Don't ask if others can do it as well as you; ask if they can do it well enough. Break a project into parts and delegate. Establish checkpoints to review what's been done and make any adjustments.
- Look for shades of correctness in your work. Realize, for example, that an email isn't completely wrong if it has a typo. It might be okay for the reason you wrote it.
- Learn from your mistakes. Some perfectionists feel if they can't do something well they shouldn't do it at all. An example of this thinking is a salesperson who'd rather work on trivia than make a call that might lead to rejection. It's better to make the call because it could also lead to a sale.

Out of doing something poorly at first, comes the experience to do it well eventually. Thomas Edison tried more than 1,000 filaments for his light bulb before he found one that worked. When asked about his failures, he said he hadn't failed; he succeeded in discovering 1,000 filaments that didn't work. Thanks to his persistence he lit the world.

Time finished: _______

To compute your words per minute: 405 words divided by your time in seconds multiplied by 60 = wpm and record on your Record Sheet under Final Read/Nonfiction.

The Flaws of Perfectionism

1. Perfectionists often measure their self-worth in terms of their achievements. True False
2. Striving for unrealistic goals heightens creativity. T F
3. "Below average" to a perfectionist is often perfectly acceptable to others. T F

4. Let your purpose for doing a job determine how much time you spend on it. T F
5. The article suggests if you want something done right, do it yourself. T F
6. In business work is either all right or all wrong. T F
7. Many perfectionists think if they can't do something well they shouldn't do it at all. T F
8. Work on trivia as little as possible and still have it be acceptable. T F
9. Out of doing something poorly at first can come the knowledge to do it well eventually. T F
10. Thomas Edison felt he failed because it took him more than 1,000 attempts to find a filament that worked. T F

PERFECTION ANSWERS:

1) T 2) F 3) T 4) T 5) F 6) F 7) T 8) T 9) T 10) F

Give yourself 10 points for each correct answer you checked and record it on your Record Sheet, Final Read/Nonfiction.

How to Remember What You Read Using Branch Recall Patterns: Don't Take Notes, Take "Pictures"

Has this ever happened: you're reading along understanding everything, and it's going so well that you keep on reading? And when you finish, someone asks, "What did you read about?" and you say, "Oh, about an hour." What you learned vanished. To retrieve it, consider taking some notes using the language of the brain.

The language of the brain

The human brain is pattern seeking, visual, and associative (try to think a single word by itself in isolation without relating it to anything else; I bet you can't do it). The brain also condenses information. So it stands to reason that a note-taking system that incorporates the elements of patterns, key words, associations, and graphics can help you remember more of what you read than a traditional note-taking system might, which is linear and uses words only. This is where Branch Recall Patterns come in.

What's a Branch Recall Pattern?

A Branch Recall Pattern is a visual representation of what you read that shows the connections between ideas, moving from the main idea to the detail. It trains you to look for ideas, uses more of your brain (words, pictures, patterns, drawing, spatial sense) than traditional notes (words only), helps you relate details to the bigger picture, and strengthens your memory of what you read.

Here's a page of notes I took before I learned to create Branch Recall Patterns. I even typed them.

The mountain is characteristically a place for Epiphany, for its position is between the mutable world of earth & the eternal world of the heavens. At the top of the mountain is a "natural tower," a manifestation of summer's perfection, and is the axis of everything, indicates a moving, a "now" to which all past time of the year has moved in growth, and from which all succeeding time will fall in decay. The sun at its ellipse, pauses & rests, before beginning its return journey.

Oneness with the external world is achieved not through meditation of art, but by direct & concrete experiences.

THE FIRST THREE SECTIONS. Variations on a theme ... the joy that results from direct experience with natural perfection. Beginning specifically in time & suggesting limitations upon it. WS moves his observer into a world of timelessness, the movement achieved principally by the indirect suggestion that the natural world is itself an artist, satisfying even the desires of the imagination, brining it to "the centre that I seek."

BEGINNING PART FOUR. Abruptly moves the reader back into a bounded realm. "One of the limits of reality ... " The poet can know a moment of complete satisfaction with & within the natural world. Then there is no need for the creative power of the imagination. No words are needed to correct the limitations of the natural world because momentarily it has none.. The direction stops & we accept ...

FIFTH SECTION. The subject is the self-sufficiency of the moment that can be properly experienced only without interference of any mediating figure between people & nature. The natural world accomplished the task usually left to the poet who is in perpetual love with the world that he or she contemplates and, therefore, enriches.

The creation of nature, of the earth & the sun, is "One of the land's children," but is also like a work of art. In its perfection all the limitations of other days of the year are both transcended & implied. This theme is expressed by the subtle & complex process of myth making that WS uses in this section, formed out of the implications of repetition. By use of parallel sentence structure, the poet suggests "one day" is somehow related to the queen.

His next sentence implies that it may resemble a mythical hero. One person becomes a race. The sun becomes a race whose characteristics are derived from it. "We are all men of the sun."

The relationship between the one & the many is built upon interdependencies, like the queen who gives birth, but who is dependent upon others for survival.

With the sun as father, and the earth mother, comes the birth of midsummer.

When nature produces such art, there's no need for people to attempt imaginative creation. They only need to look about them.

THE SIXTH SECTION. A description of natural perfection, expressed in metaphysical language. The various manifestations of summer are seen as a rock, revealing: 1) the truth promised by faith 2) the sacred stone marking the center of the earth where the seat of prophetic wisdom is located 3) like a midsummer day is a natural product of the marriage of earth & sun, rock is formed out of sediment subjected to intense heat of fire.

I had 28 pages of notes like that for one book alone—*not* reader friendly. It was as hard for me to learn from my notes as it was to learn the information directly from the book. My brain resisted large bodies of text. And we waste about 90% of our time rereading notes like these just to find the main ideas again—the key words—which are separated in time and space by all those little words on the Basic Sight Vocabulary List. So I went back to my page of notes and dressed it up a bit.

The mountain is characteristically a place for Epiphany, for its position is between the mutable world of earth & the eternal world of the heavens. At the top of the mountain is a "natural tower," a manifestation of summer's perfection, and is the axis of everything, indicates a moving, a "now" to which all past time of the year has moved in growth, and from which all succeeding time will fall in decay. The sun at its ellipse, pauses & rests, before beginning its return journey.

Oneness with the external world is achieved not through meditation of art, but by direct & concrete experiences.

1-3

THE FIRST THREE SECTIONS. Variations on a theme ... the joy that results from direct experience with natural perfection. Beginning specifically in time & suggesting limitations upon it. WS moves his observer into a world of timelessness, the movement achieved principally by the indirect suggestion that the natural world is itself an artist, satisfying even the desires of the imagination, brining it to "the centre that I seek."

4

BEGINNING PART FOUR Abruptly moves the reader back into a bounded realm. "One of the limits of reality ... " The poet can know a moment of complete satisfaction with & within the natural world. Then there is no need for the creative power of the imagination. No words are needed to correct the limitations of the natural world because momentarily it has none. The direction stops & we accept ...

5

FIFTH SECTION. The subject is the self-sufficiency of the moment that can be properly experienced only without interference of any mediating figure between people & nature. The natural world accomplished the task usually left to the poet who is in perpetual love with the world that he or she contemplates and, therefore, enriches.

The creation of nature, of the earth & the sun, is "One of the land's children," but is also like a work of art. In its perfection all the limitations of other days of the year are both transcended & implied. This theme is expressed by the subtle & complex process of myth making that WS uses in this section, formed out of the implications of repetition. By use of parallel sentence structure, the poet suggests "one day" is somehow related to the queen.

His next sentence implies that it may resemble a mythical hero. One person becomes a race. The sun becomes a race whose characteristics are derived from it. "We are all men of the sun."

The relationship between the one & the many is built upon interdependencies, like the queen who gives birth, but who is dependent upon others for survival.

With the sun as father, and the earth mother, comes the birth of midsummer. (mid-summer)

When nature produces such art, there's no need for people to attempt imaginative creation. They only need to look about them.

6

THE SIXTH SECTION. A description of natural perfection, expressed in metaphysical language. The various manifestations of summer are seen as a rock revealing: 1) the truth promised by faith 2) the sacred stone marking the center of the earth where the seat of prophetic wisdom is located 3) like a midsummer day is a natural product of the marriage of earth & sun, rock is formed out of sediment subjected to intense heat of fire.

1. truth
2. wisdom
3. purification

Did the visuals catch your attention? The boxes, check marks, numbers, star. And that's probably what you'll remember from your notes: the information you emphasized with visuals.

Then I learned how to do a Branch Recall Pattern, which looks a little like a tree branch (or a circle with lines coming off it) and is a visual representation of what I read that shows the connections between ideas, moving from the main idea (the bigger branches) to the details. I went back to my notes, plucked out the key words, and put them right next to each other on the page, which strengthened the associations. And here it is (this page says the same thing as my first page of cramped, linear notes, but it's so much easier to remember).

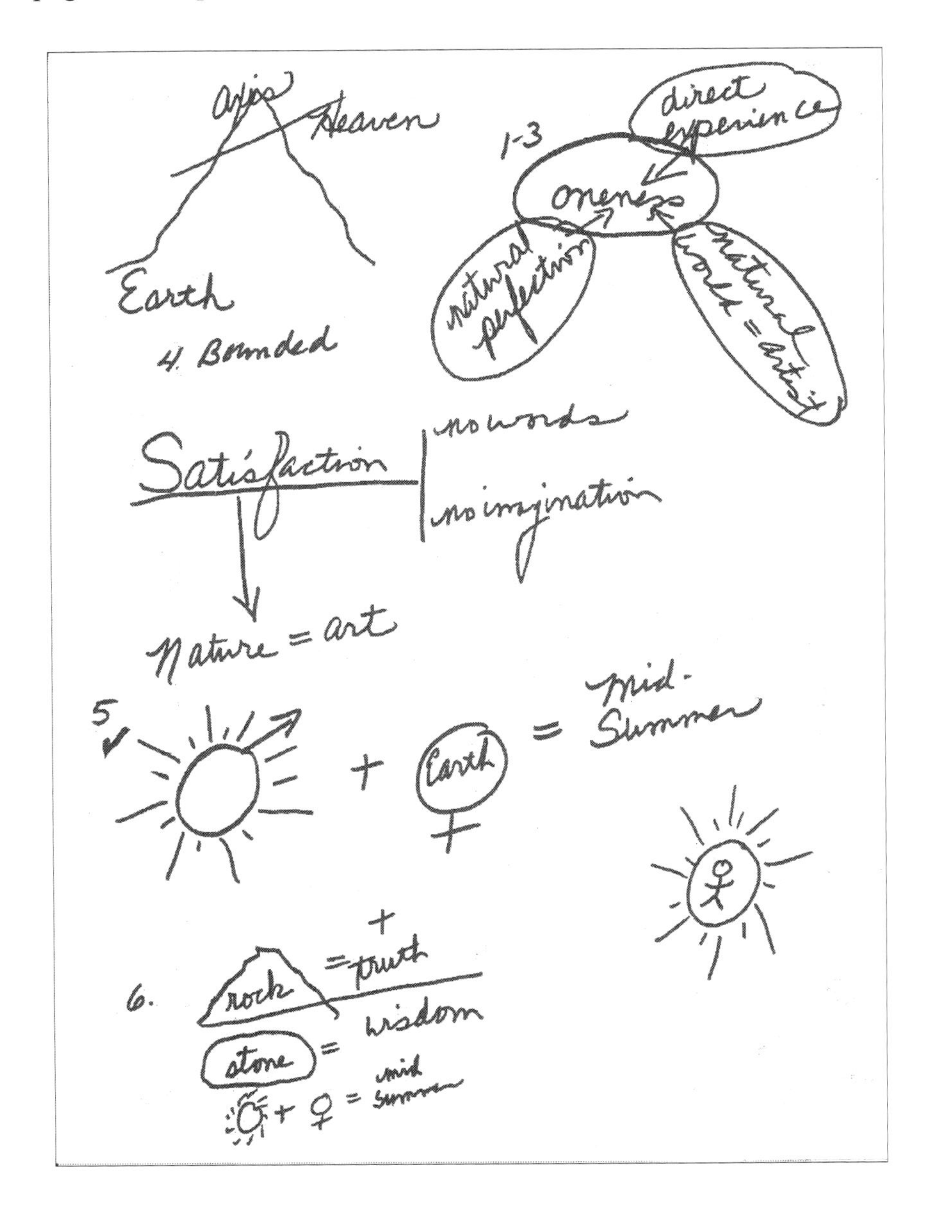

Once you remember any piece of the picture, the rest of it tends to come flooding back into your mind.

The traditional way to take notes is to list the points. You can do the same thing with a Branch Recall Pattern; just make each list look different from the others: one color ink for one list (details on the "branches"), a circle in another color for another list (details on the "rays" of the "sun"). Two lists, two very different graphics.

How to Create a Branch Recall Pattern

1. Skim through the material by article, chapter, or section before you read and jot down key words or phrases from the subtitles. Leave room to write around them. To practice "visually translating" what you read, "branch recall" short articles at first. If a book doesn't have subtitles (or very few), jot down your own subtitles with a pencil in the margins.
2. Then read the material and add details on lines radiating out from the center focus; work from the main idea to the details and link related ideas. You can also jot down your own thoughts about what you're reading and relate on a personal level to the material. This way you're an active reader, which helps you remember more of what you read.
3. Move to the next key idea and repeat the process of working from the central idea to the details.
4. Use one color of ink for each group of related thoughts.
5. Use symbols (arrows, circles, stars, etc.) or simple drawings to create a visual graphic or a picture of what you read.
6. Create a rough draft at first and then go back and polish it.
7. Create Branch Recall Patterns as you read, or read a section first, close the material, and create a map from memory. Leave the recall pattern in the book as a summary or create a folder of recall patterns of all the books you read (a "library" of sorts).

You don't have to "branch recall" everything you read, just what you want to remember in detail. And you don't have to replace your old way of taking notes, just experiment and incorporate some key words, a few patterns, and simple visuals. I think you'll like it.

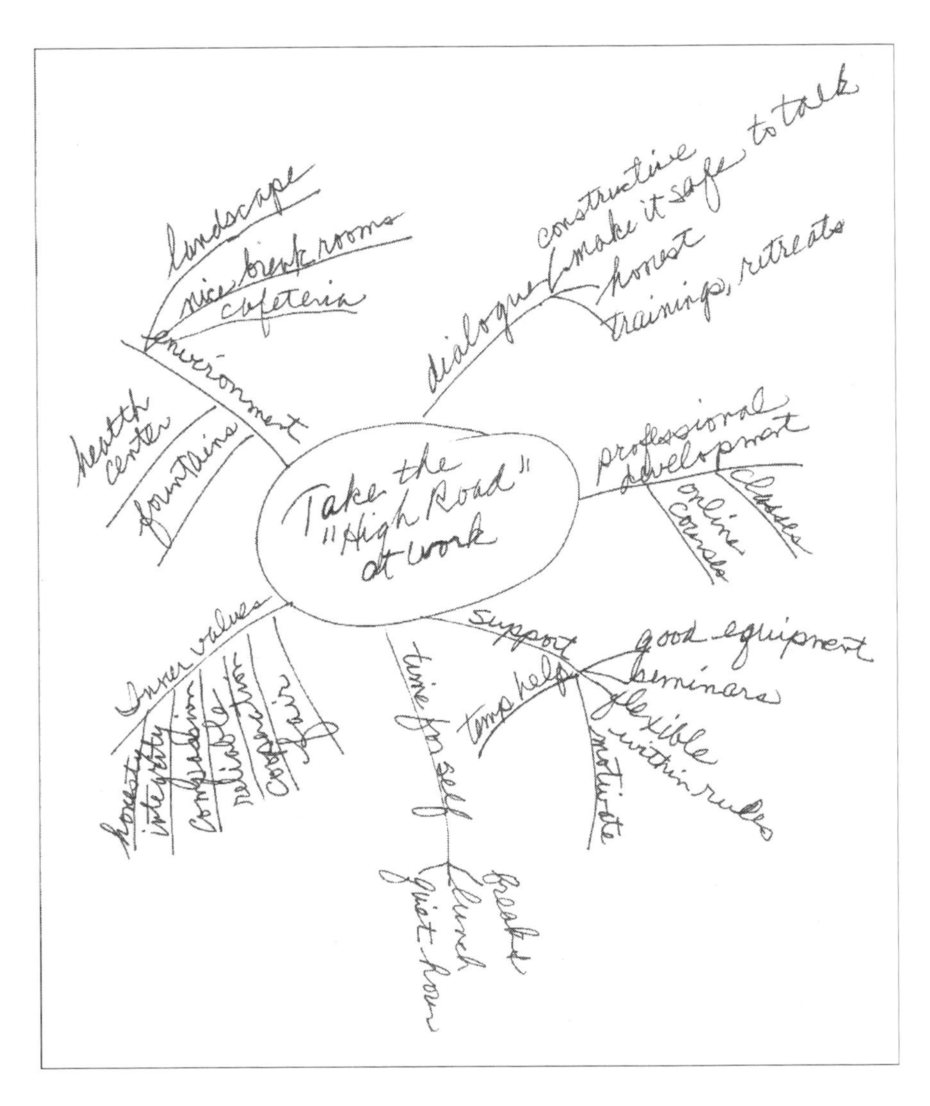

How to "branch recall" meetings, classes, and lectures

You don't usually know ahead of time the direction a speaker's thoughts are going to take so you can take more traditional notes first and then make a Branch Recall Pattern later from your linear notes.

Now it's your turn
Do a Branch Recall of the following article. Put the central idea, "Read More by Reading Less," somewhere on the middle of a blank piece of paper, and get creative.

How to Read More by Reading Less

Swamped with reading? Here are some ways to deal with it quickly and creatively.

1. **Prioritize your reading**. ***DUMP IT***. Throw out, recycle, or donate newspapers and magazines you intended to read, but haven't yet. ***DELEGATE***. Assign job-related periodicals to your assistant or team members to read; have them report on relevant information at staff meetings. ***DELAY***. Slip low-priority reading into your briefcase and read it when you have a few minutes before appointments or while waiting in line. ***DO***. After you dump, delegate, and delay, read what's left. Skim the material before you read it. A preview might be all you need.

2. **Clone yourself**. Have people save articles for you that they think might interest you so you don't have to read everything.

3. **Save warm-up time**. Every time you pick up a piece of paper you have to reacquaint yourself with it, so save warm-up time by handling each piece once. To be aware of how many times you look at a piece of paper, put a dot on it every time you look at it. Process the item before it develops the "measles."

4. **Manage by exception**. Reduce the frequency of certain items. If you ask for regular reports on absenteeism, for example, have people report to you only if it rises above a certain percent.

5. **Stay off mailing lists**. If you don't want to be on a mailing list, indicate that whenever you order something, enter a sweepstakes, or opt out of receiving further promotional material by email.

6. **Read newspapers quickly**. Most are written on a 6th to 8th grade reading level, headlines sum up the story, and everything you need to know is usually in the first two or three paragraphs. Human-interest stories, however, present more information as a story continues, so look for the gist of the article later on.

7. **Read selectively**. Information tends to be repeated, so just read two or three recent books on a topic and you'll probably stay current.

8. **Read what's left—in bites**. Divide long books and stacks of important reading into sections with deadlines for finishing each part. That way you can see your progress.

9. **Put yourself on your calendar** on a regular basis and keep the appointment; use the time to read.

How to Read Business, Work-Related, Study, and Detailed Material (SQ3R)

What's the best way to read business, work-related, study, and other detailed material? Read it several times at different speeds adding to your comprehension each time instead of reading it cold from the beginning. Here's how to dig deep into the details without falling into the hole: use SQ3R.

SQ3R

Skim and **Q**uestion
Read, **R**eport, **R**eview

Frank Robinson, a psychologist and professor at Ohio State University, developed the SQ3R strategy to help college students learn difficult material quickly and graduate sooner, and it's still used today. Let's go over the steps and then you'll have a chance to practice on your reading.

SQ3R: SKIM and QUESTION

As you skim, ask questions: what are the key ideas, how much detail do I need, what's my purpose for reading (fun, research, to learn a skill)? Your purpose will determine how fast you read and how much comprehension you want; do you need to know every chart, graph, and formula or just need to know where they are if you want to refer back to them? Then skim the introduction, abstract, summary, conclusions, study questions, charts, graphs, and illustrations to prime your mind for what's to come.

Intention determines attention.
Read with the intention of answering your questions and you'll sharpen your focus. To demonstrate this idea, take a moment now and look around the room you're in and memorize all the shades of red that you see. Do you have them? Now close your eyes and remember all the shades of blue that you saw. You remembered red

because it was your intention to remember it. The same will happen with reading. You'll remember what you intend to remember.

Skimming is crucial

When I was studying for my master's degree—before I learned to speed read—I worked hard to memorize a particular chapter. It took about two hours and I was proud of myself. And then the last two sentences in the chapter were, "We now know this to *not* be true. The next chapter discusses the current thinking." I could have saved myself two hours if I'd skimmed first.

SQ3R: READ

The first R in SQ3R is "Read." The speed with which you read is influenced in part by your "entry level," what you already know about a subject.

"You can't read fast what you can't read slow." The grammar is a little off there, but you get the idea. If you don't know anything about neurobiology, for example, speed reading won't turn you into a neurobiologist over night. You need some background in a subject to read it quickly.

If a subject is totally new, look at the glossary of the book or do an Internet search "Glossary of (whatever the subject is) terms." Study the vocabulary and terms before you read the material. This'll give you a mental database of information. You could also get two or three elementary books on a subject and speed read them. By the second or third book, you'll have a basic knowledge of the subject.

Spend a little extra time on summaries, conclusions, charts, graphs, and study questions

"Ron," a college student, thought he was having an exam in a week, but discovered it was the next day. He "crammed" for the test by studying the summaries and conclusions, answering the study questions, and reviewing the charts and graphs; and he passed the test. I'm *not* advocating cramming, I'm telling you this to illustrate the value of summaries, conclusions, and study questions; they often contain important information.

Be flexible. Just as you drive a car at different speeds depending on weather and road conditions, vary your reading speed, too, the "weather and road conditions" being the difficulty of material, prior knowledge, and your purpose for reading. Don't expect to read everything at same speed for the same comprehension.

Check new words or difficult concepts in the margins and keep reading. Usually when authors introduce new words or concepts, they define them or explain them shortly after by saying something like, "In other words," "Put another way," "Simply put," "Defined as," or "This means …" And so, difficult or new material often become clearer in the following sections. Reread later if you need to.

Take "Margin Notes." Do you highlight? It helps you to remember what you read, but can be way overdone and lose its significance. Your relationship to the material changes. You highlight something to remember it—and then you remember it—and the highlighting has outlived its usefulness, but there it is on the page throughout eternity. And something you didn't notice before now seems important, so you highlight that and pretty soon the whole page is yellow.

If you use an eReader, you have flexibility with highlighting, but if you're reading in print media consider using Margin Notes in addition to highlighting (with a pencil) or instead of highlighting.

Here's my system. I read with a soft-lead pencil in hand and put a star next to something important that I want to remember, a check next to an unfamiliar word and then I read on, an exclamation point next to something surprising or shocking, and a question mark next to something I don't understand (I finish reading the article or chapter and come back later and think about it some more).

Then when you finish reading the article or chapter, simply glance down the margins and find what you wanted to study some more. Taking Margin Notes helps you to be a more active reader.

SQ3R: REPORT

The second R in SQ3R is "Report." At least half your study time should be spent in active recall if you want to remember the material. So review your notes and report to someone, or to yourself, to test what you understood.

SQ3R: REVIEW

The third R in SQ3R is "Review." Polish your Branch Recall Pattern or reorganize it into a new pattern. Review it the next day and a week, a month, and six months later—if you want to remember the material.

"Ah ha!" How it All fits Together

Take a couple minutes to get an idea of about how much you can read in 10 or 20 minutes in your nonfiction practice material. Skim that amount for a couple minutes.

Then read quickly for good comprehension—from where you started to skim and beyond—and take notes as you go along. *Don't* compute your reading speed this time because you'll be taking notes.

Read your nonfiction material for 10 to 15 minutes and then report to someone or tell yourself what you read.

~~~

How did SQ3R, along with using Branch Recall Patterns and Margin Notes, work for you? Really well (you covered a lot of material, took good notes, and gave a great report) or you can see the potential in reading this way and you're going to give it a chance?
~~~

Those are the only two options. Either it works now or will work soon with practice. Have fun with all the techniques. It took you several years to learn to read. Now give yourself some time to get used to reading in a new, improved way.

How to Read on a Computer and an eReader

As I mentioned earlier, once you can read print faster, you'll read faster on a computer, too. And the smaller screens on tablets, laptops, and smartphones make previewing and pacing easy; just move your fingers a little above the screen.

If you read on a handheld eReader, choose a font size and screen display that's comfortable for you, advance the pages quickly for skimming purposes, and then go back to where you started to skim and read for good comprehension like you would in print. You can still use the hand motions, but don't touch the screen.

Here are some more ideas to manage computer reading.

- Use an RSS (a reader aggregator, "Really Simple Syndication," or "Rich Site Summary"). Web feed formats deliver frequently updated pages such as news stories and blogs that you specify.
- Use Google Alerts to monitor the Web for new content and to receive tailored, email updates of the latest relevant results (web, news, blogs, etc.) based on topics you specify. Track developing news stories, keep current on a particular industry, get the latest information on an event, etc.
- Bookmark favorite links.
- Block pop-up ads if they distract you.

Tame the Email Monster

Businesspeople typically get between 80 and 120 emails a day. When it pours in every few minutes, it can be overwhelming and distracting. But when you're a speed-reader, you can read anything faster including email. Here are some ideas to manage your email.

15 Strategies to Use When You Receive Large Volumes of Email

1. Scan new email "Subject" lines and delete junk mail as you go.
2. Read the last message first in a "thread." Skim the others.
3. Decide right away what action or response is necessary; this way you save time not having to reread and rethink what it's about.
4. Create email folders to sort messages by subject. Don't create a new folder for every detail or use your In-box or "Sent Mail" as a huge miscellaneous file or everything will run together and could get out of control. Sort messages according to subject, key word, or author, and move incoming, related messages into the respective folders. This keeps things organized.
5. Use filters and anti-virus programs to prevent spam.
6. Before you set up auto-filing features consider whether urgent mail might end up being auto-filed before you see it.
7. When "Sent" and "Received" items relate to each other, store them in the same folder.
8. Create an "Action Items" folder for emails that need attention. Look at it on a regular basis.
9. Avoid getting on lists for jokes, cute stories, etc. If you like to receive this material, set up an auto-filing function to send them into special files that you can enjoy at your leisure.
10. In some email programs, the "Tools/Organize" or "Tools/Rules" function lets you color-code incoming email. Use it to color-code important emails from your boss or key team members.

11. Unless you're on a team with constant hot mails going back and forth, determine a reasonable frequency to check your email. Checking it too often can be a way to avoid what you should really be doing.
12. Establish regular times to check email, like within the first two hours of starting your day so you can respond to the important messages.
13. If you have to keep records of correspondence, save your "Reply" email; the sender's email is included in the reply.
14. Use one address if you register for something on the Internet (which might attract spam), another for business, and another for personal use.
15. Regularly purge outdated and unnecessary messages.

19 Strategies to Use When You Write and Send Email

1. If appropriate, put "No Reply Needed" in the "Subject" line or the opening of your email to reduce the number of return emails.
2. Cut and paste pre-written responses to frequently asked questions (FAQs) or requests for information.
3. Do a spell check before you hit "send."
4. Put enough details in the subject line so recipients know right away what your email is about, such as "Remember budget meeting next week, 9/25, 10 a.m."
5. Have one email per subject. People often respond to your first and last questions, but overlook or forget the others, so keep it simple. Use one email to address the budget meeting, for example, another, the company picnic, and another the status of a particular report. People can respond accordingly as they have the time and the necessary information.
6. Be polite. Every email you send is a permanent record that can be forwarded to others.
7. Use plain text, short paragraphs, lines fewer than 75 characters long, and messages under 25 lines long if possible.

8. When you reply to an email, simply refer to the points made rather than leave the whole message intact so the sender has to reread everything he or she wrote to understand your reply.
9. If you forward a message, put your comments at the top rather than the end.
10. Just reply to the sender, *not* to everyone on the sender's list unless there's a good reason to.
11. Don't overuse capital letters or punctuation marks or you'll appear MELODRAMATIC!!!
12. If you don't want everyone in a group to see each other's email addresses, send the email as a blind copy (BCC).
13. Get an author's permission before sending his or her personal email to others. Then include the author's name and any necessary copyright information.
14. Don't blatantly advertise your business in a discussion group. Instead offer people something of value, such as "how-to" tips.
15. Avoid using acronyms, such as IMHO, NRN, or FWIW, which some readers might not understand.
16. Avoid using icons, such as :-P. Not all your recipients know what they mean. The same is true of using emojis, those small, digital images or icons used to express ideas or emotions. Recipients might have trouble figuring them out. For example, is that a tired face or a weary face? And is that one a worried, but relieved face or simply sad?
17. Avoid using fancy text, such as italics, bold print, colors, and emojis, which might not translate well to a recipient's screen and could appear as programming codes.
18. Prepare long attachments for easy reading: break up long passages of text with subtitles.
19. If you spend a lot of time on a computer, rest your eyes frequently: look as far away from yourself as possible (out a window, across the room, or down the hall), then close your eyes and enjoy the darkness behind your eyelids.

Insiders' Secrets and Time Saving Tips for Readers

Target your reading

If you're reading a magazine, skim the table of contents and turn to the article you most want to read, and then continue to read the material in descending order of importance to you.

Feature articles are buried somewhere in the middle of a magazine, but a lot of people read every little thing from the beginning including the message from the editor, the first article, the ads, the second article, special offers, the third article, and so on to the end. If you do that you might be out of time by the time you reach an article that interests you.

By the way, the typical magazine ratio of content to advertising is 40/60%. You could skip the ads and come back to them later if you want.

Be aware of how often information is repeated

News stories often repeat information to fill space. To see this for yourself, pick a news story and underline every time the headline is paraphrased. Also notice that the "five Ws" (who, what, when, where, and why) are answered in the first two or three paragraphs. The rest of the article tends to rehash the headline and the facts reported in the first two or three paragraphs.

This is done because if there's a late breaking story, the editor can quickly shorten the story to make room for the new material. Nothing is lost in the first news story, because the facts were reported in the beginning. So to save time if you want, just read the opening of a news story and skim the rest; you'll probably get most of the information you want by doing it that way.

On the other hand, "human interest stories" and "creative nonfiction" pieces in newspapers often use literary devices, such as mood, imagery, and anecdotes to create factually accurate narratives. The facts are sprinkled throughout the story so you can read these articles as you might read a short story.

Know how stories and examples are used
Stories and examples are used to clarify information or entertain the readers; this is fine, but sometimes they're used to bulk the material, too. Authors often have great ideas, but don't always have *long* ideas. What would you do if an editor told you to turn in a 65,000-word manuscript by the first of the month and you were 3,000 words short? Might you be tempted to pad the manuscript with stories and examples? Might you make your point and then add, for example, "Sarah does it this way in her office, Jamal does it this way, and Aaron does it this way." *Hmmm*, still 900 words short. "And Ramon does it this way and Marcus does it this way."

It's true that people remember a few well-placed, poignant stories better than dry information, but an overabundance of stories and examples might be more for an author's convenience than yours, so skim through the parts you don't need. The exception would be an anthology like *Chicken Soup for the Soul*, which is a collection of short stories that relate to the central theme of the book.

How to Read Smarter

Magazines and Journals

1. Target your reading according to importance, and then skim each article (Wave, Slant)
2. Read summaries and conclusions first; that might be all you need to read
3. Read with a purpose so certain facts catch your attention
4. Read using the reading hand motions (Brushing, Tapping)

Correspondence

1. Prioritize your mail: dump, delegate, delay, do
2. Skim (Wave, Slant) to find out *who* wants *what* by *when*
3. Read using reading hand motions (Brushing, Tapping)
4. Choose a course of action and follow through

Newspapers

1. Skim the article (Wave, Slant) and then read (Brushing, Tapping)
2. News stories: look for who, what, when, where, and why in the first 1-3 paragraphs
3. Feature articles and human interest stories: look for additional information as the story progresses
4. Editorials: suspend judgment until all the evidence is in

Novels

1. Skim before reading (optional), then read using reading hand motions (Brushing, Tapping)
2. Strive to understand the characters' behaviors, motives, joys, sorrows, and goals
3. Look for symbolism and universal truths in the story

Nonfiction, business books, and textbooks

1. Skim one chapter at a time before reading it; if it's long and exceptionally detailed, skim part of the chapter before reading it
2. Read for good comprehension (Brushing, Tapping)
3. Use SQ3R

Speed Reading Guidelines (Summary)

1. Let your purpose for reading (for research, to get an update, learn a skill, read for fun, or simply be aware that the information exists if you might need it again later) determine your approach, speed, and level of comprehension.

2. Speed read all nonfiction, work-related, and detailed material (that you want to know and remember) using SQ3R; read more slowly, if you want, only *after* using SQ3R.

3. Skim by chapter using the preview hand motions, the "Wave" or "Slant" (unless you're reading a who-dun-it novel or maybe poetry) and then read for good comprehension using the pacing hand motions, "Brushing" or "Tapping."

Will you enjoy reading this way?

For me speed reading was like avocadoes. When I tasted my first avocado, I wasn't sure I liked it, but I thought, "That's interesting. I'll try another." And now I eat them regularly. Think about something you didn't like as a kid, but love now. Mushrooms? Coffee? Booze? They're acquired tastes. Speed reading might be an acquired taste, too.

Also remember that most of your work-related reading isn't great literature. For example, look at your inbox; anything in there you want to read over and over and savor? You probably just want to get through it.

Speed reading is an option

Now that you know how to speed read, you can choose to read quickly or more slowly. But you must decide, because if you don't, you could backslide into slower reading since that's the way you've read for years. Every time you sit down to read you might want to imagine a switch in your mind. Flip it "up" when you want to read fast and focused for great comprehension and be sure to use the techniques you've learned in this book.

And that's it

Congratulations! You now know everything you need to know to be a faster, better reader and you have the tools to increase your concentration, memory, and comprehension.

Have some fun with it. It took you several years to learn to read. Now give yourself some time to get used to reading in a new, improved way.

Be upbeat, "I read quickly and comfortably … I focus well … I look forward to reading … my comprehension is great … I finish my reading in record time and I remember what I read."

All you have to do now is follow through.

How to Continue Your Progress

Fun, Informal Drills

1. Practice your speed-reading skills on magazines in the grocery store while you wait in line to check out at the cash register.
2. Speed read your kids' books so you know what they're studying in school or reading for fun and you can talk with them about it.
3. Pick a new subject that interests you and speed read three elementary books about it to get a basic knowledge of the concepts and vocabulary.

Structured Drills Step-by-Step

Aim for speed first to practice understanding at faster speeds (drill on material for which you ***won't*** be held responsible). Then when you return to your regular reading, of course you'll read for good comprehension (remember to skim first), but because you practiced your speed drills, your day-to-day reading should be faster than you used to read.

The drills help you to relax and begin to understand larger amounts of material effortlessly. This dramatic increase in speed and comprehension can take anywhere from a few hours to about three weeks of daily practice.

First practice in easy novels; as you become comfortable with the techniques choose more difficult books. Practice every day. Start from where you left off in the book the day before. Work your way through a book like this. When you finish one, begin another.

Drill 1

Mark off a 10-page section. Skim the whole section for 1 minute, read the same section for 2 minutes, then reread it for 5 minutes, compute your words per minute (wpm), estimate your comprehension, and start a Branch Recall Pattern. **Repeat the drill two or three more times**, increasing the number of pages by five each time. **Then, from where you left off, *skim* as far as you can into the book for 2 minutes** (new material) and then *read* that same material for good comprehension, compute wpm, estimate comprehension, and add to your recall pattern.

Drill 2

Skim into your practice book as far as you can for 5 minutes, look for key ideas—who, what, when, where, why—and mark the place where you stop. **Skim the same section two or three more times for 5 minutes each** (finish the section at least once and, if you finish before 5 minutes are up, skim it again). This gives you a sense of how it feels to read at a skimming rate. **Skim into the book as far as you can from where you left off** (new material) another 5 minutes. See if you can cover even more pages this time and understand what you're reading at the faster rate. Compute your words per minute and estimate your comprehension.

Soon you'll be eager to forgo the structured drills and "press on." That shows that the drills are working. Now you can speed through books and enjoy them, no timing or repetition necessary.

Speed Reading Software

You've learned everything in this book that you need to know to greatly improve your reading rate and comprehension. If you'd like some exercises that automate certain drills and rapid-perception training you might want to use the software described on my website at WinningSpirit.com/speed-reading-software.

Full speed ahead!

Bonus Reading for Fun, Information, and Practice

The Three Styles of Readers

If you're basically a **VISUAL READER** you interpret what you read through mental pictures. You can learn to speed read fairly easily unless you let a descriptive phrase send you off into a daydream, which is okay—just be willing to sacrifice some speed and maybe some comprehension. Your challenge is to avoid becoming too involved in the images the reading inspires that you slow down. It should be fairly easy for you to learn to speed read.

If you're basically a **VERBAL READER** you interpret what you read with your intellect. You're comfortable with ideas, new concepts, and abstract subjects. Because you love words you might be concerned you'll miss something important if you don't pronounce every word to yourself. Your challenge is to ***not*** look too long at every word. You can still "wallow" in your reading, but now that you're a speed reader you have an option: you can choose to read some material quickly and some more slowly.

If you're basically an **EMOTIONAL OR FEELING READER** you interpret what you read through your feelings. You can become so emotionally involved in what you're reading that you risk becoming mired in details. Your challenge is to keep the big picture in mind.

Whatever your style of reading drill in material for which you *won't* be held responsible, which removes any initial anxiety about missing information.

Also drill in easy material first. When you were learning to read, the words in your storybooks were large and few and far between. Speed reading isn't the old way of reading speeded up, it's a new way to read. So practice some every day and then, because you practiced, your regular reading will be faster naturally.

"Photographic" Memories

An eidetic image is a precise visual memory of something that was seen. Only about 2% of adults have *fully* developed "photographic" memories. I've found, however, that speed reading tends to improve people's ability to visualize. You might want to practice the following exercises—in addition to speed reading on a regular basis—and see how you do.

1. Select an object or scene. Glance at it, look away, then glance at it again for 2 seconds; notice patterns and colors, and look away. Glance again for 5 seconds, notice the details, close your eyes, and remember it vividly. Glance again for 2 seconds, close your eyes, and remember it. Later, bring it into focus in your mind.
2. In your mind move an object, rotate it, zoom in until it fills your mind, and then shrink it to the size of a grain of sand. Do this several times.
3. Look at the layout of a printed page as though it were a picture. Close your eyes, remember the subtitles, size of the print, the spaces; mentally turn the pages and watch them in your mind imaging you're understanding effortlessly.
4. Skim a magazine or book, close it, remember phrases, words, and pictures.
5. Before you resume reading a book, skim what you already read to practice skimming.
6. "Frame" something to remember: mentally flip a "switch" to signal when you want to start to remember, then when you want to relax your attention again.
7. When you look at a photograph of a landscape, focus behind the picture and imagine that you stepped into the scene.

Your Four Vocabularies

A "vocabulary" is the total number of words you have at your command.

1. A speaking vocabulary is usually the smallest of the four; about 1,000 words.
2. A listening vocabulary is probably larger than your speaking vocabulary because you can understand words you've heard before even if you're not familiar enough with them to use them in conversations.
3. A writing vocabulary is probably larger than both your speaking and listening vocabularies. This is because when you write, you can mull over your choice of words and consult the dictionary if necessary.
4. A reading vocabulary, the number of words you recognize in print, is probably the largest of your vocabularies because you have the context to help you figure out what new words mean and the dictionary in which to look up definitions.

Four Ways to Enlarge Your Vocabulary

1. Learn the common prefixes and suffixes to help unlock the meanings of unfamiliar words.
2. Learn "synonyms," words that have similar meanings, and "antonyms," words that mean the opposite.
3. Make a list of new words and their definitions and study them whenever you have a few extra minutes.
4. Read books on topics that interest you, but which are fairly unfamiliar.

Directive Vocabulary: Reading Road Signs

Imagine you're going on a long road trip. The weather, road conditions, and terrain all dictate your speed. You drive faster on dry, straight freeways going through flat areas, slow down winding your way through cities, be extra alert following detours, and use caution going through the mountains.

Likewise vary your reading speed—even within the same article or chapter—according to the "conditions." A preliminary skim will give you an idea of your entry level (how familiar you are with the subject), the difficulty of the material, and how the author uses stories and examples ("drive" faster if you understand an author's point and don't need to labor over the stories and examples; slow down if you want more clarification).

The following words and phrases are a different kind of "road signs" that also give you valuable clues as when to speed up or slow down.

More of the same is to come (continue your current speed): •Additionally •Also •And so •Another •Furthermore •Similarly •Likewise

Clarifies or explains what an author said (continue current speed or speed up): •For example •Specifically •Such as •For instance

Defines a term used in the text: •Defined •Simply put •In other words

Emphasizes (continue current speed or slow down): •A key issue or concern •Above all •Without question •No doubt •Of course •Certainly •Particularly •Clearly •Especially •For this reason •Significantly •Important to note •The fact remains •Obviously

Summarizes or concludes (slow down to study the author's conclusion or, if you understand it, speed up): •Accordingly •In short •Thus •As you can see •In retrospect •Basically •To summarize •Consequently •Last of all •Most important •Finally •The bottom line •In conclusion •Therefore •To reiterate

Reverses thinking, says the opposite, makes a contrast (these words weaken the ideas that precede them; prepare to change your thinking): •Although •If •Rather •But •In contrast •Conversely •Instead •Unless •Despite •Nevertheless •On the contrary •However •On the other hand •Whether or not •Otherwise •Yet

Indicates a list or series of steps: •First, second, third •Some benefits are •Some reasons are

When to Read Sidebars

A sidebar is a block of text that contains additional information not covered by the main article or chapter and is set off by a border, a larger font, colors, or other graphic elements.

You're likely to encounter 13 kinds of sidebars in your reading. A quick skim before you read lets you know what kind of sidebar you have. Here they are, "In roughly descending order of prominence," writes Greg Daugherty, author of *You Can Write for Magazines*, a book I highly recommend. Greg was my editor when I wrote a time-management column for *Success* Magazine.

1. The "Useful List" Sidebar adds information related to the main article, which isn't necessarily covered in the article. These are often "bullet points," key ideas. Read these before or after you read the main article.
2. "Not-Especially Useful, but Interesting." Fascinating facts. Read after you read the article.
3. The "Quiz" tests your knowledge. Take the quiz before you read the article to see how much you know about a subject or after you read the article to see how much you learned.
4. "Terms You Need to Know." Key terms used in the article are defined and set aside from the main article. Read these sidebars to acquaint yourself with the terms before you read the article.

5. "You can Do it, Too." Tells you how to do the same thing—or something similar—mentioned in the article, such as going into business for yourself or grooming your dog. Read this after you read the article.
6. "Where to Go for More Information." A list of resources if you want more information; keep for future reference.
7. "Questions to Ask." For example, ten questions to ask in your first interview, five questions to ask your teens before they go out with friends, etc. Read after the article.
8. "What to do if it Happens to You." What to do if you win the lottery, have your identity stolen, etc. Read after the article.
9. "It Happened to Me." This personalizes information in the article by sharing the author's experience. Read it when you're curious.
10. "Meanwhile, Elsewhere." Gives readers a sense of the trends and the bigger picture beyond the scope of the article. Read after the article.
11. "Q&A." Allows you to explore in greater depth issues in the story. Read after the article.
12. "Recipe." Read this before you pull out your pots and pans.
13. "It Didn't Fit in the Main Article." Read after the article.

Mr. Daugherty concludes by saying, "The sidebar may be a small canvas, but it can also be a masterpiece."

When to Read Footnotes

Footnotes are explanatory notes, credits, references, and sources listed at the bottoms of pages that refer to information on the pages on which the footnotes appear. They contain references the author consulted or referred to in the main body of the text, direct you to useful information that pertains to the subject in the text, or give credit for a quote or information from another source

A quick skim before you read helps you identify how an author uses footnotes; from that you can decide when to read them according to what information you want from them.

Eye Relaxation Techniques

1. **Far focus**. After reading or doing close, detailed work, change your focus to a distant point. Blink naturally and breathe deeply and comfortably several times to refresh yourself.
2. **Palming**. In this popular Bates technique, cup your palms over your closed eyes and lean forward comfortably, resting your elbows on a table or a desk in front of you. Enjoy the soothing darkness behind your palms.
3. **Beach ball**. With your eyes closed, imagine a beach ball in your hands getting smaller and smaller; and then toss it away. This technique, recommended in the book, *Superlearning*, helps to dissolve tension.

Reset the Clock for Free Time

Peter "The Time Man" Turla
www.timeman.com

How long is your workday? According to Parkinson's Law, "Work expands to fill the time available for its completion." The more time you allow for work, the more work you find to do—and keep doing. All of which does nothing for your home life or social life. You might love your job more than anything, but if all you do is live and breathe business, you're probably missing out on some valuable, life-enriching opportunities.

Whether you're making time for your family, continuing-education courses, or just for yourself, here are a few suggestions on how to seize some moments of self-renewal.

Your family: Nowadays many family members shy away from togetherness in favor of "doing their own thing." When this happens, they become just a group of people sharing a house, rather than a family.

- Don't wait for free time to open up magically so you can do something together. Have regular planning sessions. In addition to going on special excursions and vacations, plan household projects to tackle together. Rather than have one person work in the yard while another cleans the kitchen, have everyone work in the yard until it's done. Then move inside and do the household chores as a team. Appoint a captain to oversee various projects and rotate assignments so family members can interact with each other in different roles.

- Schedule TV time rather than sit through an entire evening of random programming by default. Have a reason to turn on the TV, and turn it off when the show is over. Don't watch TV during dinner. Reserve dinnertime for family sharing and enjoying each other.

Continuing education: Explore new subjects or take classes to further your career. For each hour in the classroom, expect to spend at least two or three hours studying. Plan time for lab work, conferences with professors, and commuting as well as regular study periods.

- Optimize study time: record lectures and listen to them throughout the week. Spaced repetition helps you file the material more quickly in your long-term memory.
- Take seminars or online courses as convenient alternatives to semester-long classes.
- Study in 20- to 40-minute increments with 10-minute breaks to think about what you learned. The longer you study without a break, the greater the risk of forgetting. Avoid all-night cramming sessions. Study throughout the course and review at regular intervals.
- Explain why you can't work overtime on certain days, why you might need some time off during finals, and why you appreciate quiet time to study. People will respect your goals when they understand your goals.

Yourself: Spend time each day doing what you want to do. Read, listen to music, pursue a hobby, or just sit and think. You don't have to occupy every moment of the day with work or activities. To free up some of your valuable time at home, consider the following:

- Combine activities. Turn exercising into a social event. Walk with a friend or join a health spa. Play music or listen to your favorite talk show while you do routine chores.
- Group errands. Plan meals for the week and do your grocery shopping in one trip. Drop your clothes off at the cleaners on your way to the grocery store. Know the best times to go to the store, cleaners, and gas station; when they're least busy.

- Reduce time you spend on chores. Eat in a restaurant occasionally, pay your teenager—or a neighbor's teenager—to mow the lawn, and hire someone to clean your house.
- Turn off/pause/put away your smartphone/cellphone and other electronic devices while you're resting.
- Avoid overextending yourself. Learn to say "no" and make an effort to work within the limits of your time and energy. Work on tasks that will bear the most fruit. Learn to compromise; most deadlines can be negotiated at least a little. Know how much work you can handle and plan realistically.

Time is a limited commodity. To better manage your life, better manage your time. To better manage your time, plan and schedule each day.

You don't achieve a significant life by wishing. You achieve it by scheduling your time effectively, balancing your professional life with a rewarding personal life, and living according to what you value. If you plan to have a high-quality life, have quality planning. Protect your precious time and energy. What you choose to do today is going to cost you a day of your life. Make it an equitable trade.

###

Made in the USA
Lexington, KY
02 December 2019